ALL THESE FIRES,
AND NIGHT STILL DARK

Iraqian-born, Parisian-based, **Abdul Kader El-Janabi** set off, at the beginning of 1970, for London and after two and a half years, left to Paris where he settled up today as a French citizen.

He founded in Paris, in 1973, *Le Désir Libertaire,* the first surrealist Arabic review, banned in the Arab world for its critical approach to social and religious issues.

Author of many collections of poetry and essays, a translator into Arabic of many American and European poets such as Paul Celan, Blaize Cendrars, Miroslav Holub, René Daumal, Joyce Mansour, William Carlos Williams and recently an international anthology of prose poem, Abdul Kader El- Janabi has also published into French many anthologies of modern Arabic poetry. Most of his surrealist poems are included in his *A Horseback Afternoon* (Broken Sleep Books, 2022).

In his *The education of El-Janabi* (Journa inactuel de l'oubli, L'Asymetrie 2024), he retraces his route to the frontier of different cultures. He now runs *La Revue de la poésie in toto,* a magazine dedicated to radical poetry.

Also by Abdul Kader El-Janabi

A Horseback Afternoon   (Broken Sleep Books, 2022)

Contents

ISBN: 978-1-916938-43-4

Cover art: 'morte mea, speciosa" by Aaron Kent

Edited and Typeset by Aaron Kent

Broken Sleep Books Ltd
PO BOX 102
Llandysul
SA44 9BG

All these Fires, and Night Still Dark

Abdul Kader El-Janabi

Broken Sleep Books

There is a poem down there,
In the air castle of the barricades,
In the wreck of prose,
At the funeral of the muse,
In the folds of nonsense,
In the blasphemy, the nobility, and the rage
At the bedside of the rhyme.
The poem is a drum
At the whim of the madmen,
A dodo bird, a coin for the outcast.
The awareness in a moment of desolation!
It is wherever

> Reason is on its knees,
> Sufi is annihilated
> And all senses are active.

The poem is always a whizz
That does more work than noise.
Its glory is not in the acclaim,
But in its transient bloom
Breaking through,

> Once and for all,

The comprehension of the world!

For Aaron Kent

I break prose into poems
        Like wood into a pyre.

Figures and symbols
        Shape a mind
                That gives birth
       To presences, men and suns of images
Fashioned so precisely
        That they arouse desire
                Along the syllabic line of memory

Nothing remains
> But deeds,

Shadows of a shade

Speaking a language

Of bullets and birds

Fell already

From the other side of the brain.

No one can equal

No one can hear

The sky is too high
> For the dead

Wedged down the field.

Let your memories spread
                        In the open
                And allow what is bubbling
Beneath the surface
        To flow under the poet's lids.

Neither
        Of us
                Is a witness.

                        No flesh between the wing and the dead.

Make a comet-like exit
        To flame off in the sky,
        To blaze tomorrow
In the vocabulary field,
Wherever swimming goes against the current,
Where there is no comma
Between range and horizon.

And there, only there
Open your records
And let the birds come from long journeys
        To digest their wounds.

Gain your speech,
Be silent when others speak
    To hear yourself speacking.
                        You perhaps know who is beneath,
But you don't know who is above.

What did they give you
        When you came into the world?
Nothing.
Only instincts,
Eyes
And feet to tether you to the heap.

For how many cold dusks
Did they leave you draped in fog?
While the firmament was dying down
        Over their heads.

Do not seek the truth,
Take it from the horse's mouth.
Don't write your life down,
        Scribble it,
                And the song begins
Right through you.

It detects your movements
Relates the future of your thoughts blooming.
Don't lose it. You need it, like
A frozen light, in the bottomless well of undesirable words.

At nightfall you're an action.
Shine then only in your obscurity.
Don't worry about a specter that wants to protect you,
For a tainted slumber has swamped all:
   Your playground, the path, and glittering rails.

Your fate struts, impels you
Before it discloses its shore
In this blue deluge,
Where the bombardment revives the wound;
And opens a window
                To what so ever
Makes what's dormant, utter,
And roar like a city
        Lined with open mouths.

From which grass did you come?
On which stele will you carve your name?

How many tears remain hanged on the lower palpebra
                And now are sacrificial?

At home, you are deceived.
 And outside, defeated.

Hunkered down in your spleen.
Looking within yourself.
        All that is left for you to express yourself,
Is the neutral zone.

Yet the winter is coming
To warm you to go off at a run
With its breath and fire.

Your sin is inevitable.
The moon denounces you.
In the gateway wind,
        Only bright dust can make sense of you
And flare its grains scattered in these elegies
        Which look forward to your ear,
            To poetize them.

For long, times were colorless.
Nothing to trust, but your skin.
To each sense,

A night,
        A share of vision.

Neither haze spurts into your eyes
                Nor the stone exhale its strength
Into the orbit.

No flame to choose you.

Let your power of will to be here and now
      Move along the barricade's edge,
Since a block of thought stands
Between you and the mystic star.

Take a mouthful of evergreens;
For the image shields itself.
It becomes valid only when it is spoken.
In the message of the desert,
A severed tongue is written,
      Leaving only ash on the page.

Here is your history.
It throws you in its can of oblivion
And in a gesture of setting a good example,
      It commits suicide.

And when the divine falls asleep at night,
And the chiefs take up his dreams as arms,
You make a covenant with a bomb blast.

In the event of a winter snap,
War will serve as your warm coat
And pandemonium will erupt like sparks.

The voice, down your body,
Whispering in dark caves
Calling the moles to come out!

What is the inspiration for the poem,
                   This crime of infinite joy,
To be commited.

The city creeps along
    The eyes of the poet
Branching off
Into a row of hazy mirrors,
Crowded lanes
    And scattered leaves.

How hermitic is this dominion
Filled with aerial creatures
Rising above the tall building
        In the form of a tree
                To defend the sinful beauty.

It has a shelter inhabited by the rain
Protected by the torrent-rise of hesitance
When the sun sets, to define
The way to home.

How simple to see simultaneously
The rise of a new world
        And its collapse
On the very blank page.

        Inspiration?

Since then,

        Banal is divine!

By a miracle of childhood,

   Fast roots,

With flames

   Strewn down the page to remind,

Loomed in the night,

Drew closer to

   The moon

In a mad vortex,

   In the grove

     Where the swallows

      No longer have a family

To take them on a wild ride.

Over the inner cliff,
> A dying dove

Abandoned to the wake
> Of mental obsession,

Ready to anticipate nights
Surrounded
> By feline auroras.

The rain will come ere the rooster crows.

Face your distant destiny.

Morning is rising for you.
Every hour a new cycle
Every wing a new shade,
Every street is a path
       To the one, you were mourning.

Your heart still beats.
Your tongue is free.
No shadow in the vastness,
Since what is hidden has no sense.

See, all that you see
It grows in the lap of reflection.

You weep for no one and, no one mourns for you.

You are a crowd in your loneliness.
Memory is the vault of heaven
From which trees and odd bits,
The sweat and the night
       Are flowing.

Names drip with mysteries,
Falling from nowhere,
To be deciphered in the stone garden,
In the cells of the brain.

If reason, in your view, is the seed of sunshine
And heaven is your inheritance of wonder,
Pray then
> For the thin line
> Of this ethereal shrine of nature,
>> Sacred to be tide up with a whine.

What will tomorrow bring?

If not a scar, a trace to testify

Without eyelashes,

A journey,

A desert

And that thing

      Which

         Always

            Runs away

Leaving nothing but traces

With no refuge

In its apparitions

Except this fissure in the book

Through which

      A past not mastered

Looms with the very fabric

Of words clenched in anger.

What will tomorrow bring,

If not, this grass

Doomed to be straw,

A yellow dust

On slushy ideas,

What, If not,

      A body that blooms under a new light?

There I lived in Baghdad
The fragile city of my first years,
Years of running with no guilty conscience,
Toward revolt from all sides.
Where are you now,
                    At this moment of plotted rill?
                                            How can I write you,
From the balcony to the water, taking you back
To seasons more remote than the two rivers,
To air-conditioned theaters and concepts,
To bookshops and sidewalks boiling with backstreet dreams
Where I supped the boundaries in shaky gulps.

O my illuminated city
You, whose face rubbed with bullets,
Used to radiate at sundown
Shattering the roofs into shadows and reflections,
While we were searching for the light of the north
          To record the time in hours,
          From morning to morning,
                    In filthy notebooks.

In those years bodied with hope despaired already,
One got the urge to invent imaginary windows
Through which the stranger may infiltrate and subvert,
And, in exchange, we enter his reaches for a breeze.

O my raft, stranded in the harbor of theory,
Of the shining knot, nothing is left but foam.

No dawn, no mint... to open the kernel, the omen.
The poets are still in their comfort zones.

If they had only slept on the bed of a stream, far-off,
Time wouldn't hold back from leading us
To a sesame, **open O poem**, originating new beginnings.

Tide rises, emotions are huge
And resistance is blind.

What can I do with a memory,
Which cannot be but a memory
What can I do with a past which is afraid of births
Living only in the depth of those who have gone,
And dying only in the land of the living.

A bird
An eye
And a child of the rivers.

Between space
And the bark of the trees
Birds die alone,

Giving off a shimmering reflection
Of a noble angel
Often
        Asleep

In the formation
Of hell

In the crevasse
Of decay.

If ever the ship sinks

If a sibylline song rises in the air

If that which is in vain, misty, and rough prevails.

What flash of lightning awaits,

What revival for the lost

Without beginning!

Heads have been drawn to the foot of the forest
Hands have broken through all the mirrors
That failed to promise the wandering soul a sudden chill
A bundle of organs has collapsed
Upon the waterlines of the blade
When Sven Malvin was born
To keep the traits of the human shape
Before it disintegrates
Into a parabolic wood.

For Sven Malvin

Learn to speak without words
To describe with blanks
What happened to you.

Tie language to your bed.
Close the doors behind it.
Don't let it run away.
It's your beam,
        Your caster in the gambling
Who rolls the main.

At this infinity,
Bides your new-born silence.

At the body of this death
The word moves up and down.

And ah, we poets,
Why is our testimony supposed to be the terror
                    That is hidden in the written word?

It surrounds us constantly and everywhere,
As if it were a marvel.

Is it the instinct we live by,
            The other *us*,
            Down the time to be born and die?

Terror that is the footprint of you and *i*,
The resurrected ghost of words
Serving those who are caught by the language hands!

It shines from every direction,
To propound that:
            To write is
            To see Instantly:
That the sublime is in the ephemeral
            And that the antithesis is in the glance.

City without radiance,
Plunged into the dark
> Where the wind and the sun
> Consume everything.

A white city
> Stained with Cain's blood,
Where beauty
> Sips winter sap.

Like the birds who nest
Among tall branches in full bud,
Wholeness
                    Is evaporating
                Into the threshold of a doorless infancy
Preserved by lines of yearning,
Like a source of fleeing dawns
                        And menacing midnights.

Eternity beholds you
While you lie calmly on the ground;
Its eyes shine for you in the distance.
As a diabolical light's defiance.

Only the shadows can trace their ancestors
In the embers of absence.

We shall raise the torch
And keep a monotonous rain
So that your body can slink
Out of the horizon pain.

Nothing left for the sleepwalker to proceed to
Except the flimsy sheaths,
The agitation of what goes on in the head,
The blood, the flesh,
The mud and the clay.

Like dead fishes, the details will resurface.

How cobwebby is the body of the poet?
Swimming against the tides of its never-ending
      Speechlessness, it battles the estuary.
It sails through in the stillness,
Not without feeling, dislike, or feverishness.

Its solitude,
This cruel piece of dignity,
                           Explains the riddle of ignition:
      The eternal is desire.
      Spiritual hunger is tenebrosity,
      And those movements which decrease in a safe place
      Are nothing but holy waters,
So, the creature and the stone
Perform ablution.

No doors, no dials,
Only the gap of your life.
You shine in the walk
You absorb everything you see
Like a lake upon which
Your part of pain sits as a watermark.
The mystery is your only link
All words click in your mouth.
The rhythm is too fast.

In these hours, time descends into sleep,
Dreams create the world
That you sense in yourself,
The world that often hides
   Below slumber.

Give it its map, its skin
And its buildings, borders.
Its thoroughfares and coffeehouses.
Give it
   Its lost sun.

You should mirror first, then move
To the subject matter.
Perhaps its rays make you feel light-headed.
All the birds have flown in disarray
And in the crypt,
That great forgotten ship within you,
Hope found its place of safety.
Space deciphers the mourning of the storm.

You only grow to be akin to your own words.
While, at the edge of the road,
Numbers fly around,
You'll feel the saliva of "*there was light*"
Which declared the world.

Scrolls will entrust us
>With the details of your descent to earth.

The sun will open
Your morn ruffled by emotion,
And your sail will blow
Towards the very first depth of the sea,
Taking you on a circular walk
Around the white marble of a philosophy
That bows before your little house
Like a mighty star
>>And the waters hence absorb you

In the blue visibility of the night,
Where the dead hit the hay.

Roots and syllables
Names and dates
Sands and sea spray.
Here are your tenant reflections
In the winter diary, to bleed!

Graze on words from another world,
The stuff of visions,
And deliver your soliloquy.

For all the lamps in the world
        Can not
                Illumine a place
          Inhabited by loneliness.

Let fall your robe,
>Sister of the night.

The owl of Minerva
>No longer,

>>>>While dusk falls,

Spreads its wings!

Hegel, shadowless, opened history
>With the saliva of dialectics.

She is dead, the poet's mother!
She no longer lifts her two vague veils,
Her eyelids!

Overwhelmed with daydreams,
Her son wanders under the foliage
Where angels once passed,
Watching a parade!

A collapse of memory,
Rhetorical clashes,
Words-in-freedom
      Running in zigzag
          Giving shape to his image.

Yes!
The poet's mother
      Is dead
And with her,
          The moon!

You are already on earth
Listening to the fall of sounds
      In the paradisal ponds of
the void.

You were born to play,
And, in life, one must play
Happy or sad.
Play and play on without
inhibition

                         Until the world's first hours,

Until the foggy tail-ends of
dawn
When your memories start to
crackle
      With blossoms
Facing powerless state of
mind!

In the fog,
　　　　No memory
　　　　　　No spark. Light is a slab, in the shadow

On a bridge across the bank
Where my doppelgänger is in sight,
I find myself
　　　　Face to face
With my faiths,
　　　　　　My madness,
　　　　　　　　And
　　　　　my
　　　　　monologue
　　　　Drilling holes in the
unsealed sky.

On my ruins I shall walk
> To your hair

Where the word, opening spontaneously,

Releases seeds growing in line
> With the limpid movements of the mind.

I shall walk

In the blend of the absence
> With the seaweed of the first call

> Scratched in time,
>> And locked in a book,

To breathe the elation

And the freshness of intellection
> At a moment of dance!

In a fertile landscape
Man/woman
They each design his own effigy,
His pagan mirror,
Through the the frontal depths
of which separates them

They each find his alchemy
      In the eruption of mutism,
            In the feeling of ecstasy!

Yet, in balance,
It is still language that delivers
      And rides the flow of boredom.

The oil splashes
As a shade at noon.
Halftones and targets
Playing along with a brush
      That eases the mind
In the oval commonplace
Where imagination has slipped
      On the rinds
         Of its form.

O thou, son of the image,

Set your efforts,

And float through the ocean.

Be immediate, an archer

To hit the target, offshore,

Where the accents swim disjointed

As meanings

Drool over rings

Of light.

Don't say, "Where's my bread".
Your rising sign
>Contemplates the face
>of the rock,
>Reflects fair skies,
>Drives out emotional
>fervor,
>Goes out without a
>lantern,
>Shines like coral in the
>field,
>Ends the toil of
>divination,
>In the dark that lurks
>Behind the door.

With no death, no beach.
Between seeing and prophesy,
Words, always, exceed themselves,
To reach the shore.

Kill your self, poet!

Those faces which come into view
To rake the past of the Word
That has kept us on a string,
Those sources of the unvoiced towards which
One always directs his steps of mind,
Those silhouettes in the light of the cave
Smoothly sway to the magnet of time,
Those talks, cries of the useless,
Nightish suns
   Unfurled.
Those with spears
Watching for those who have none.

At the edge of the abyss

As far as the eye can see.

A man,

A tree,

A wind.

And

A poet in between.

A bird of prey
        Whose feathers
        Carry furs
To a distant tree.
Under the bow of his eye
        The branches shiver.

A bird of prey
Chokes in his entrails
The fledglings of the landscape.

Only silence can see him.
The silence that stretches
Like an oar
On the river of divination.

It is over your shoulder now,

       The new world. Catch it

              Like a fly

  And explode yourself,

     In the grass

     Reverberating

On the sidewalks of the road.

And all that comes from the North

Leave it on the side of the bed.

When the night
Dreams of Ibn Khaldoun,
Consummation occurs
In the earth's mouth
Between the rivers and the breeze:
                    Sand grain,
Seed of thought.

To Aziz Al-azmeh

Poems come forth
Soundless
Like blows
That the mind repulses.

A line lost and found,
   On a sheet of paper
Almost blank, stretches
Like body and soul
Shimmering its own aloneness.

In the floods of the book,

      At the distant edge of the universe,

         Near the lush alley,

            Four floors from the stars,

I saw you stretched out,

          Cherished through disclosure,

    On the bed of the river

Above the glimmering waters,

Making love to the waves

While the night went by

        Without moon.

You were looking for the bird,

        You once fed

Leashed by fury,

        And now has fled.

A kind of sculptor, that you were, a sheverdess

Sipping, drop by drop, from the reservoir of elements.

Raw desires

      Guard your inner self.

No fears, no ghosts...

You make love with a pure lust for timelessness

As a syllable on its way to the line.

Since you're fame in the night,

History will shine upon your thighs

And recline along your stature

        As a sign of wisdom.

You resist the lies of the mind

In the heave of the orgasm,

Letting your body groan with pores dripping

Echoing vertigo and insomnia

And when asleep

Your muscles relax in a frentic silence of ecstasy

                    Bringing any pangs of frustration under control.

Under

Earthlight,

      In a magnetic field,

    The orfic figure

    Sings

        To the poets

          Of the skeletal

           Wave

             On rampart.

Take the lamps to the universal table.
Their drowsy shadows,
       Creepy in the late hours,
The wind shakes them
       On edge.

The human statue
          Which grows as beauty for all
     Is on tiptoe
       Before slipping into
       The high forest of a coma,
Tending the waken storm towards dreams.

Beneath the mirror's rinckles
The murky riddles of your past
And the smiling rhizome of your no tomorrow,
Strip off Eden's tree,
      And of Word's remnant, left underneath,
        Forge a vase of flowers,
For your window of a seer.

Hope walks blindly on the roof of prediction
Spewing blond smoke into the air.

A mist fogs the place
Within the debates
Where we were
In the company of flowers
   Springless,
   Sleeveless
Like an entrenched enmity
Between revenge and oblivion.

Hope
   Still turning in,
At midnight.

         It is always there
   Playing in the heighlights
Caring little for our fate knotted in the dark.

The apparition   of Ezra Pound   in the crowd   :
An orb   on a wet, smoky   photograph.

Would they have worn out
All senses,
All curiosity,
All support, all pear-sized bees,
And all the things with
       Holes in time?

In those hollow cellars
While the night
       Was falling to dust
              Over our primal ancestors,
Darkness binds a curtain,
That veils the sun,
Forbidding the block of time
From melting into
       Space along the line.

In the name of the night,
          Of hunger and hope,
In the name of place and principle,
In the name of all those who died,
In the name of the youth,
In the name of borders
          And barbed wire in the flesh.

The noble Cause visualizes a land
On a dark wind of dreams.

Between the outpouring of days
And the shooting of the camps,
Between the fruits of summer
                              And the breaking of the winter
Between the epics of the decision
And the refusal of normalization,
          Death, too, has its carnival:
                    Streets in flames
In the name of nothingness.

Unable to pray!
I am more vertical than
       The minaret!

Me,
   I advance in the light.
It,
    Cracks, immobile
In its secular obscureness

Did it happen to you
Skulking in an alley
      At a late hour,
Casting a shadow
      Over stray cats of the cosmos,
Mouth-open like a gorge
        Of a god stripped in sleep,
With no bite to eat
      Apart from Numbers
      Shattered
In words on words,
        So, lip to lip, they meet?

It was raining in Baghdad
Suns and moons
Meanings and images.

A lamp flickered in the air
       With a juvenile blaze
Between Tigris and Euphrates,
The straw of our intellects
       Is enflamed.

History, like a Sufi in search of nectar,
Flew away in pursuit of its own time,
          To remain tragic in its course.

In a culture where lovers preferred
       Fleeting pleasures,
The gazes of the movers were trying to catch,
       From the cell's windows,
          A glimpse of the far-off place.

It was raining
       Alternations and cobblestones.
But, the birds of the great river
Rarely flew
       After sundown!

To Alphonse Girard

It is not the time for suicide:
The balcony is high.
The air is polluted.
And the stream of death
Hates splashing.

Life is a pet
Which has no wish to go down
                    Into a mire of beings.

Then plunge into the water
            And the iris will carry you
                        To the bosom of the earth.

Streets split out
       From a small square.
Buildings line each lane.
Each prismatic windowpane
Reflects a far-off tree
       Covered in gold leaf
That is falling to the ground.

It's always

      The same reader,

      The same poet,

      The same woods!

Time flies, and we are hungry and thirsty.

      Let us slay

      These caravans,

      And go back to satisfy

         Our yearning to flay

What remains of their words.

That's how,

      The first hour drinks

      In silence,

From the basin of the day,

Without waking the whole night.

That's how

          It rises and advances

Without shade nor shred of a ray,

Slipping on the crust of all these instants,

Falling from the depths of nothingness,

Flying instants that time claims.

That's how

Without frightening

Either the night

      Nor the dawn

Nor the divided bird.

That's how,

                Under a stream of light,

Solitude falls

      Interminably

In the air of the time.

Defiantly, the sun rises.
Would lids devour their eyes?

I escaped to the mouth of the night
Climbing the staircase of exile.
Dust phalanges
Leaking out of the mesh of the hand.
Summer shivers.
Its clouds drown in the eyelid of the day.
A star shook horizon's hand.
I see it in the victim's heart,
It approaches like a precipice
Roaring with hats,
Like the crows of the horizon
Hovering in the glow of caution.
The twilight would march to a farthest knocker.
From behind the wheel,
Houses are springing up around me
The air growls in the calm of lightning
Dancers mow down soldiers
And here comes epilepsy and its haze
So low they cross your eyes
Then a black insomnia
Bleeding red flags
Break the back of the street.

Future garbage comes out
        Of wagons plenty of ideas.
The unbelievers are tossed
        By the winds of belief.

In a few moments
I'll write it down.
In a few hours,
Tomorrow for sure,
I shall write it.
In a year,
In a few months,
In a week,
But I will pen it.
In ten,
A hundred,
A thousand years,
I'll write this cursed poem,
So that it represents me
On the day of judgment
While I honor
    A charming harem girl.

Which word was the first uttered

      In the Garden, I wonder?

When was it?

      Before the fig-leaf or after?

      And who utter it?

The snake,

      Adam

         Or Eve?

No evidence, beneath the tree.

In this luxuriant jungle of automatism
Should I continue to speak of the diluvian sleep
Which has become a conquering force?
The solitude of the night pushes me to deflower
The wet burgeoning of the dream
Where my bones rest.

From the cavities of the dawn in its petrified black size,
New forms emerge, a shell of love
Moaning in the bed of a distant river.

Thus, the ghosts follow one another.
Then from each mouth comes a murderous shadow.

In the torrential night
A vase becomes a child's mask
Doubt wove for me calm fugues
Lifted me to the flames
Of my members.

No measures
To fill you with profane rainbow.

The real-world is an abandoned balcony,
An optimism, a hand in the sun,
It buries a sea hidden in the creasing
Until the archive of the lips,
        Where vision feeds on idols,
Of a sky under which I walk.

Discovery is only a tree that grows without water.

Here is the morning, shaken by the mystery,
Eagle of a hidden distance,
Galloping through the gorge of the fog
Devouring a ravine in the heart of the night,
In the heart of nowhere.

It is a light morning with woolen fingers
It reveals a new hazardous memory
Requiring from me reflexes on the run,
A look capable of insinuating itself
In the corpse of answers,
In the prisoner veil of doubt.
Fuzzy flight unceasingly insurgent
Such as the joy of the rivers when they carry away
The menstrual period of the visible erudition.

Everything tries to hatch,
To become solid on fragile islands

The distances collapse on water needles
Shattering and flying away
Burdened with the pushing of words,
Eyelashes and swords.

What simulates death
Before this dove leaning on the shoulders of time
Guarded by the witch of the village
Who wears the dress of death
And whose silhouette is terrified?

Any answer is a skull that rises from the ashes

From a tombstone
And offers me the present in all its laziness,
A summer bubble that I explode in the void,
A refuge from madness to the hostile feelings,
Scatters of the cry in the form of corpses,
Frustration exhausts them in the fire of days.

The ebb and flow of the shadow makes the mirrors palpitate
The sun treads them.
And the temporary madness of generations
Flows from their face.

So is the man, a smoke melted in the dizziness,
He seeks his way in the mud of noon
He endures des ailments waking up at the top of the horizon
Covered by the stones of a future distance
There, his being collides with the bullets
Coming from the mouth of the law
That these or that lands have imposed.

Man is but a spirit suspended
In the omen block
Behind the doors of the defeated
Where the eye of a boy shines
Staring at the commands of the wind.

By a clever progression
He finds himself plunged into the ditch of dates
Invaded by laughter and trembling
And so, he repeats the game of renewal

Which establishes a new map in the head,
A map with no phoenix, or excessive desire
But carries in it the pride of revolt.
The prophecy I receive is a phoenix,
Comes out of the eye of the needle,
Bursts, naked, between the commas and the signs.

It is time to move to summer pastures,
To descend the steppes of existence
Where the body is unbuttoned light,
                    A word against the current.

No longer a baptism of words.

The poem is androgenetic,

Between stopped time and the rising rhyme,

Between night and the candlestick,

From antithesis to the immediate,

It forges the coin and animates the

ambivalence.

As if the mind were a beach,

    A coral island caught up

        In an analogical sea.

Words do not make love any more.

They are spirits,

They want the secret,

The sentence, under their sky.

Image is an amalgam of language.

With thought, it becomes a slippery ground.

The word falls, orphaned

            Like a rattling leaf.

The poet collected the carcasses of his

language

           Hung in his study room,

And ran with the tidal bore of a river.

I was on a journey
To the world
      Of William Carlos Williams
Looking for the null
      Of all equations.

I went looking for
          This *surface effect,*
In all the notebooks,
      In the back streets
That's past all-seeing.

I was on a journey.

I got lost!
      The variable foot was:
Centrifugal, centripetal!

And now,
How to sum up the journey.

I get up early.
I have breakfast.
I get ready in front of a mirror
In its reflection, vertigo unfolds
In images that captivate my attention:
Books invade my room,
The dead whose names I have forgotten,
The Mashrabiyas of Baghdad,
The street I cross every day,
The incessant ballet of the promiscuous women,
The crowded grocery stores,
The movie theaters,
The burst of hailstones.
And when all is mixed up
I recover my balance!

We have to accompany
The poplars to their roots,
Weaving light clothes
To a buried darkness.
We are here, there
And everywhere the reaches are open to us
And the stars prepared to weigh us
With a forbidden fruit.
We are natural born decadents,
Playing with words is our luxury drug.
With the goal of discovering another birthplace,
We can hardly ever impart wisdom.

Still immaculate,
In the sky
Our shielded dream.

Freedom

Has been contrefeited into a name
And got lost in the color of the dust.

Yet, what we keep in mind,
Is a scar with a sunflower,
And a flame subjected to
The law of the day.

Once upon a time   In the ancient East
There was a waiting room...

Lo!
The migrant bird behind the doors
We no longer hoped for his recovery
So much rigor and distrust did he show.

But this passionate lover
Who had a Christian upbringing
Had sometimes dreamed of glory
Which gave imagination a finer edge.

The migrant bird
Rises above the conventions...
That is the secret of his proper sound.

Sin had tattooed him with its crazy blessing.

He scattered the remains of the sun
In the depths of the seas
Where the mirrors discover the burrows
That shelter the fledglings of words.

In a certain way
The blood of the climate flows
The mirror-idea hung on the wall of the poem.

A chain of fear.
A In blatant indpiration, a grey matter is detained.
The world is language.

Swayed by a stormy sleep,
The migrating bird
Ran in the alleys of the glance

Three children were playing
He greeted them with warmth
Then threw them into the river
And as if he had fired stray bullets
All the passers-by became birds

The bird took refuge in the desert
Whose only inhabitants were
A severed head,

        Sand

            And a sunrise.

Anciently, the poets will be.

To Ounsi El Hage

In a vision, I saw poets

                    Inviting drunk words

To share their libations in a pub.

As soon as they sat together,

They all started shouting and yelling

While the adjective dogs were peeing on the rugs,

                    Verses were leaking out,

Sheets of paper were flying overhead.

Fans applauded whatever they heard.

Copies were distributed,

                    Journalists promised to blacken pages.

                    Publishers rearranged their folders,

And suddenly, all faded away leaving the universe

                    Rainy, gray, still, and silent.

Yet nobody had ever seen the poem.

It had locked itself in its room

Waiting for the silent moon to alight on a bough.

Now that all to begin again.

Along the hedge of blasphemy

The delirium of the murderers' flowers

Exhale a smoke of eternities, infinities.

Time loosens the grip of age

        Dragging the days over its shoulder.

An idea clogged by

        The whisper of a utopia

                Confounds all ears.

The stowaways leave the enchanting dwelling

And fall in a successive movement.

        On the highway of becoming!

In the reaches, the ceremony begins.

A voice from the past:

No Beauty,

                              Its wing is a metaphor.

Our houses are too far,

      Language can't help.

         Words gone beyond bounds.

Hesitantly,

Over that blank page of poetry's history,

An image has navigated

> To let words, settle illegally in a sentence
>
> Ringing the bell of calling

Like a glimmer in a rift.

The poem,

> Extracted from elsewhere,

Keeps our eyes peeled.

Men who — I did not know — descending
To the underworld of a bear hug
To meet the invisible woman.
Men, haunted
        By visionary, flaming aims.

These men,
Born to fill the pages with torment,
Are begotten by women
Adorned with the phallic smile of forbidden books,
Women expel from their navels
The birds of simulation
Delivering the secrets of their temporal life.

The night is so indigo
That the earth seems like a chalice
Of water troubled by a drop of ink.

While a fresh soul
Was thinking of complying with eternity,
It shone brightly as soon as they met!

The time before a rendezvous with my bed:
In an absent manner I remember things.

My chair is barking beneath me
A shoal of fun minds my wrist
And the hailstorm headlines my nobody.

I am a tiger of languages
Contemplating in a jungle of dictionaries.

Wandering in despair
I saw the blond girl whose nightie, made of insomnia,
Infringing upon the caper of laughter.
I can get nothing out of her gingerbread
Which is melted like a cirrus
In the Nomad's mouth where I generated
The experience of lost nights.
I was anguished
I moved to the abyss of things
Hoping to knock the Nation over.

I rushed into the street
And it was dark like a piece of ice.

I didn't have a knife
But before you could say knife
I skinned Time off.
Taking its flesh and bones
Making of them
A barbarian full of ardent shrieks

Having no equal in snaring a look
Nor in denting a passing smile.

I released him hovering on the mountains
Where dreams lurked everywhere.

And then on returning
He could not find the way
And fell into deep discouragement
Smoking his last bun of nexus.

I retraced my steps
Went up many times
And not seeing how to get out
I fell asleep,
Instantly waking to him
Vomiting his own flesh
In a vessel of darkness
And he told me
        « You will find here what you seek»
And disappeared.

A dream house
       Under a roof of natural color.
Upstairs, a window with a crumbling sill is open
       In the shape of a suitcase.
The entrance door is closed.
In front of it, a child is chewing at a book.
In the street, a hooded shadow swings.
It is the silhouette of the guardian
In rude confrontation
       With ghosts rushing
              Out of the keyhole.

Trees with faded leaves,

A square with an opaque vegetation,

Cemeteries free of chimers,

A daybreak dipped in fog,

Salaried words

    Whithout the sadness of a whale

      Nor the joy of a shark.

    Reality will not close its last page,

    And triumph will get no chips on its shoulder.

In company with our chimeras
We rise from the depth of a tragic act
Carrying
         Joy,

                              Knowledge
                AND
Light.

                         *

Day
                Is
                              Another night of awakening.

While language sighed in a closet,
The deserter of all exercise,
      Brushes the pierced tongue of a young word.

It's time for him and for the poem
      Dressed with verbs and nouns,
            To wake together
From a deep sleep of reality.

At homme,
In a courtyard less obscure,
Poetry is near the door,
   Pulsing with rage and nostalgic line.

Like a locomotive
In a world without a call of the wild,
The poet of breathless line
Remains present
Wherever a stand looks over
      A swath without an epilogue.

His life, (as in life),
      Hazards a new world
Between a notional and the normal definition of life

          Each new verse comforts his cup of coffee:
He no longer watches the hogwash going high
And his readers keep asking for something sweet
    To dream about.

A man sleeps
In a field.
>His glasses
>>On the grass.

A meter away,
>A girl fondles her thighs
Looking at the sun.

Suddenly
The sleeping-man
Fidgets,
>Starting to look for
His glasses:
Colored clouds are dissipating.
>No more oil.
Whiteness dominates
>And there is no longer light!

>>>Then the sleeping man dies

Accumbent
>As a long
>>Colored
>>>Stain
In the artist's painting.

Books, writing table, colored pencils.
>Near an oil painting hung above the fireplace.

A man opens a bottle.

The ambient light

Pushes a patch of darkness
>Towards the outside...

From a corner, the music rises

And intermingles with the noise.

Smiles. A lady wears a black dress

With sad nostalgia.

She laughs,
>Saying

She has come from afar.
>A visitor

Picks up from the ground

Her purple shawl.
>Whispers.

Near the front door,
>A man tells a story.

Suddenly a glass breaks,

Startling the people.

Silence.

The noise returns,

And then it fades away
>Little by little,

The gloaming begins
>Gleaming

>Through deaf forms
>Among which

I was searching:

A shift in his vision
Made him whisper:

Where is the signature?

All of a sudden,

In the sun set of darkness,

> The grave opens itself.

The moon

> Lights up, for the assassins,

> > The way to their target.

Acknowledgements

Special thanks to Sara and Rupert for their proof reading and precious suggestions.

LAY OUT YOUR UNREST